Amanda Gorman
Poet & Activist

by Grace Hansen

Abdo
HISTORY MAKER BIOGRAPHIES
Kids

abdobooks.com

Published by Abdo Kids, a division of ABDO, P.O. Box 398166, Minneapolis, Minnesota 55439.
Copyright © 2022 by Abdo Consulting Group, Inc. International copyrights reserved in all countries.
No part of this book may be reproduced in any form without written permission from the publisher.
Abdo Kids Jumbo™ is a trademark and logo of Abdo Kids.

Printed in the United States of America, North Mankato, Minnesota.

052021

092021

Photo Credits: Alamy, AP Images, Getty Images, iStock, Panos Pictures, Shutterstock PREMIER,

Production Contributors: Teddy Borth, Jennie Forsberg, Grace Hansen
Design Contributors: Candice Keimig, Pakou Moua

Library of Congress Control Number: 2021932416
Publisher's Cataloging-in-Publication Data

Names: Hansen, Grace, author.

Title: Amanda Gorman: poet & activist / by Grace Hansen

Other title: poet & activist

Description: Minneapolis, Minnesota : Abdo Kids, 2022 | Series: History maker biographies | Includes
    online resources and index.

Identifiers: ISBN 9781098208882 (lib. bdg.) | ISBN 9781098209025 (ebook) | ISBN 9781098209094
    (Read-to-Me ebook)

Subjects: LCSH: Poets--Biography--Juvenile literature. | Poets laureate--Biography--Juvenile literature. |
    African American women poets--Biography--Juvenile literature. | Women activists--Biography--
    Juvenile literature. | Feminist poetry, English--Juvenile literature.

Classification: DDC 928.1--dc23

Table of Contents

Early Years

Amanda S. C. Gorman was born on March 7, 1998, in Los Angeles, California.

California

Amanda and her twin sister Gabrielle were raised by their mother, Joan. Joan was a 6th grade English teacher. Amanda shared her mom's love of reading and writing.

Amanda had a hard time speaking as a child. She worked through it in **speech therapy**.

Education

Amanda attended New Roads school in Santa Monica through 12th grade. In her senior year, she earned a college scholarship.

Amanda went on to Harvard
University in Massachusetts.
She studied **sociology**. In 2020,
Amanda graduated *cum laude*.

13

Works and Awards

In 2014, Gorman became the first Youth Poet Laureate of Los Angeles. The next year, she published *The One for Whom Food Is Not Enough*. It is a collection of poems about hunger, community, and other important topics.

SOCIETY

A SUSTAINABLE

FUTURE

raising awareness
on human dignity,
respect and equal
opportunities

15

In 2017, Amanda was named the first-ever **National Youth Poet Laureate**. That same year, she read at the Library of Congress. She performed, "In This Place: An American Lyric." It is about how every person can create change.

On January 20, 2021, Gorman became the sixth and youngest poet to read at a **presidential inauguration**. At 22, she recited her poem, "The Hill We Climb" for the country.

Gorman added more to her list of works in 2021. One includes a picture book called *Change Sings: A Children's Anthem*. People of all ages can be inspired by Amanda Gorman and her words.

Timeline

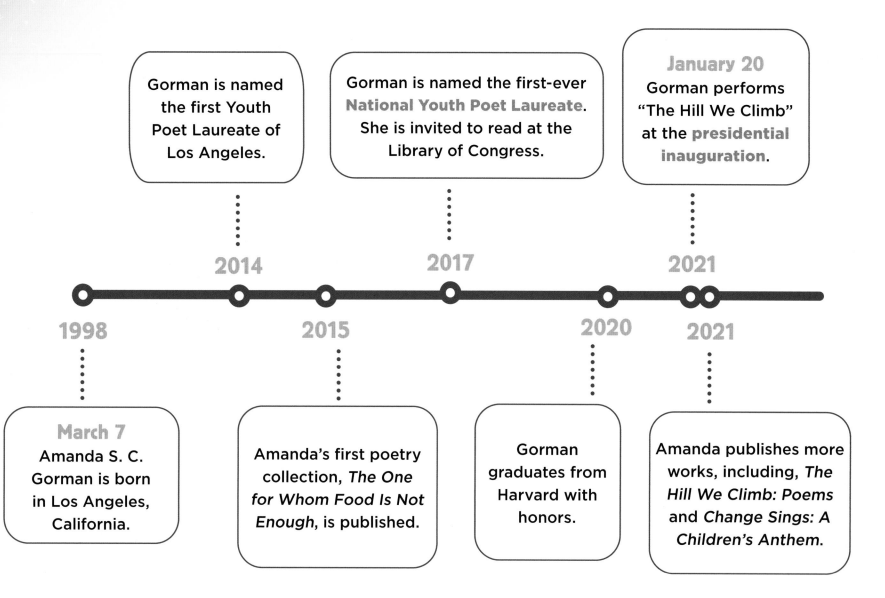

Gorman is named the first Youth Poet Laureate of Los Angeles.

Gorman is named the first-ever **National Youth Poet Laureate**. She is invited to read at the Library of Congress.

January 20
Gorman performs "The Hill We Climb" at the **presidential inauguration**.

2014

2017

2021

1998

2015

2020

2021

March 7
Amanda S. C. Gorman is born in Los Angeles, California.

Amanda's first poetry collection, *The One for Whom Food Is Not Enough*, is published.

Gorman graduates from Harvard with honors.

Amanda publishes more works, including, *The Hill We Climb: Poems* and *Change Sings: A Children's Anthem*.

Glossary

cum laude – a Latin term meaning "with honor" and used to indicate good academic performance.

National Youth Poet Laureate – a title held in the United States by a young person who shows skills in the arts, particularly in poetry and/or spoken word, is a strong leader, and is active in their community.

presidential inauguration – a ceremony to mark the official start of a new four-year term president of the United States.

scholarship – money given to students to help pay for their education.

sociology – the scientific study of human society, like its origins, development, organization, and behavioral patterns.

speech therapy – training to help people with speech and language difficulties to speak more clearly.

23

Index

Abdo Kids
ONLINE
FREE! ONLINE MULTIMEDIA RESOURCES

Visit **abdokids.com** to access crafts, games, videos, and more!

Use Abdo Kids code **HAK8882** or scan this QR code!